HISTORIC
COMMUNITIES

Colonial Life

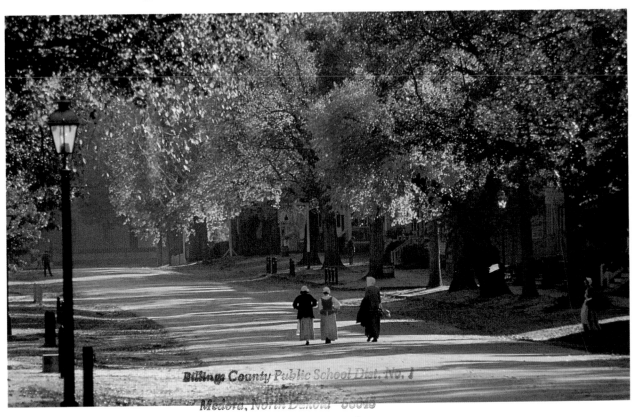

Bobbie Kalman

 Crabtree Publishing Company

HISTORIC COMMUNITIES

Created by Bobbie Kalman

For my daughter Samantha

Illustrations
Cover and inside art by
Antoinette "Cookie" DeBiasi
Pages 9, 13, and 26 (top) by
Barb Bedell
Page 31 by Karen Harrison

Research
Carlienne Frisch
Jodi Gaspich

Editors
Carlienne Frisch
Shelagh Wallace

**Story "Celia's family" was
written by Samantha Crabtree**

Design and Mechanicals
Antoinette "Cookie" DeBiasi

Color Separations
ISCOA

Printer
Worzalla Publishing

Photographs
Courtesy of the Colonial Williamsburg Foundation:
Cover, title page, page 5 (top), 6 (top), 7 (top), 8, 9
(top), 10 (bottom), 12 (top and bottom left), 14, 15
(top and center), 16, 17 (both), 19 (left), 20, 22, 23, 24
(both), 27 (both), 28.
Peter Crabtree and Bobbie Kalman: 5 (bottom), 9
(bottom), 10 (top), 11 (both), 12 (bottom right), 15
(bottom), 18 (bottom), 19 (all three in right column),
21 (all three), 25, 29.

Published by
Crabtree Publishing Company

350 Fifth Avenue   360 York Road, RR 4   73 Lime Walk
Suite 3308   Niagara-on-the-Lake   Headington
New York   Ontario, Canada   Oxford OX3 7AD
N.Y. 10118   L0S 1J0   United Kingdom

Cataloguing in Publication Data

Kalman, Bobbie, 1947-
  Colonial life

(Historic communities)
Includes index.
ISBN 0-86505-491-6 (library binding) ISBN 0-86505-511-4 (pbk.)

1. United States - Social life and customs -
Colonial period, ca. 1600-1775 - Juvenile literature.
2. Slavery - United States - History - Colonial period, ca. 1600-1775 -
Juvenile literature.
I. Title. II. Series: Kalman, Bobbie, 1947- .
Historic communities.

E162.K35 1992   j973.2   LC 93-30206

Contents

5   The first colonists

6   The other newcomers

8   Colonial homes

10   Settlements to towns

12   Questions and answers about colonial life

14   The colonial family

16   Celia's family

18   Children at school

19   Children at play

20   Men's clothing

22   Women's fashions

25   Travel, transportation, and taverns

26   Work and fun

29   Stories and songs from Africa

30   Prejudice

31   Glossary

32   Index

Map of the Thirteen Colonies

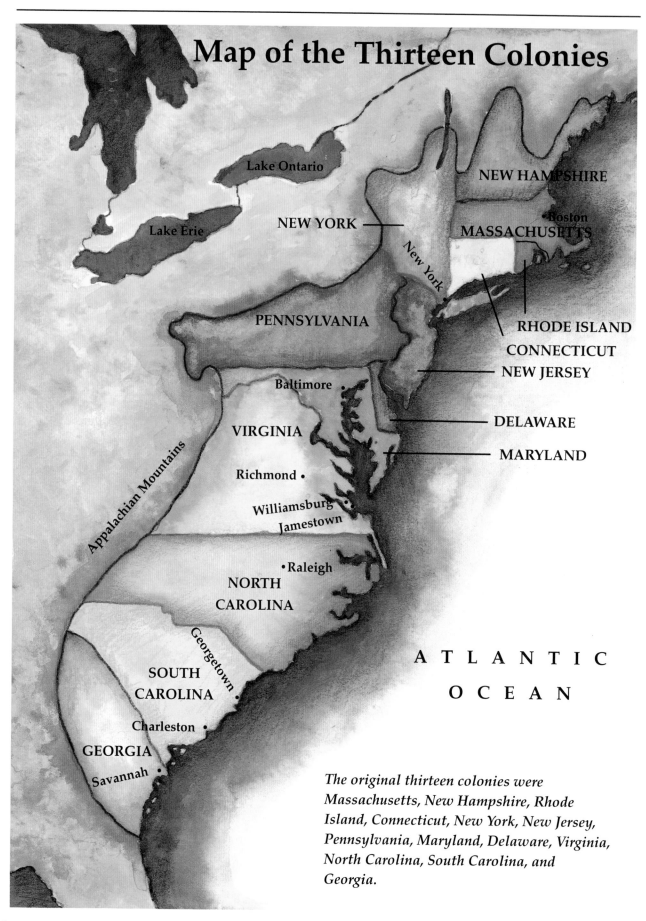

Lake Ontario

Lake Erie

NEW HAMPSHIRE

NEW YORK

Boston

MASSACHUSETTS

New York

PENNSYLVANIA

RHODE ISLAND

CONNECTICUT

NEW JERSEY

Baltimore

DELAWARE

VIRGINIA

MARYLAND

Appalachian Mountains

Richmond

Williamsburg
Jamestown

Raleigh

NORTH
CAROLINA

Georgetown

ATLANTIC

OCEAN

SOUTH
CAROLINA

Charleston

GEORGIA

Savannah

The original thirteen colonies were
Massachusetts, New Hampshire, Rhode
Island, Connecticut, New York, New Jersey,
Pennsylvania, Maryland, Delaware, Virginia,
North Carolina, South Carolina, and
Georgia.

The first colonists

About four hundred years ago, small groups of European people sailed to North America to begin new lives. Some were looking for adventure; some had been sent by their kings or queens to claim land for their home countries. Others wanted to be free to worship God in their own ways.

Settling the new land

Settlers came to America from Spain, England, France, Holland, and Sweden. In 1496, a group of people from Spain became the first European settlers in North America. The first permanent English settlement was established in Jamestown, Virginia in 1607.

The settlements in the New World were **colonies** of European countries. The people who lived in them were known as **colonists**. They were still considered citizens of their faraway countries and obeyed the laws of those countries.

The Thirteen Colonies

As the new land became more settled, people continued to arrive from Europe, especially from England. The settlements quickly grew into towns, and other settlements sprang up farther inland. In the southern colonies, farmers became wealthy from growing tobacco, cotton, and sugar cane on large farms called **plantations**. News of great opportunities brought thousands of settlers, all hoping to have better lives in the New World. Eventually, the colonists formed the Thirteen Colonies that later became the first thirteen states.

The first settlers came over in sailing ships such as the ones in the picture. These ships can be viewed outside the historic fort of Jamestown, Virginia, the site of the first permanent English settlement.

Most of the settlers were men, but sometimes groups of women sailed to the New World to marry the men who were living there.

The other newcomers

Not all the people who came to live in the colonies were from Europe. Many thousands of men and women were brought from Africa to work as slaves on the plantations. Plantation owners needed large numbers of workers to help them plant, cultivate, and harvest their crops. They could not find enough workers in the colonies, so they began buying black men and women from Africa to work for them as slaves.

The slave trade

Some people believed that there was nothing wrong with kidnapping, selling, and owning another person whose skin was a different color. **Slave traders** sailed large ships to the coast of Africa where they bought native Africans from people who had kidnapped them. The slaves were chained and crowded into the lower decks of the slave ships. On the voyage to America, many died of starvation, suffocation, or disease.

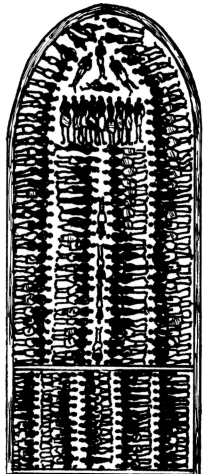

This diagram shows how tightly the slaves were crowded together in the slave ships.

Plantation slaves

Most of the slaves that were sold to the plantation owners worked with crops. They were called **field** slaves. Field slaves worked from sunrise to sunset. They could stop to rest once a day for fifteen minutes. An **overseer** in charge of field slaves punished them if they stopped working. Some collapsed in the fields from working so hard in the hot sun. ·

Small chances for freedom

After the first black slaves worked for a number of years, they were given their freedom. The governments of some of the colonies, however, passed laws that took away the rights of African Americans and forced them to be slaves for life. Slaves could not legally marry, keep their families together, own property, or earn their freedom.

Some plantation owners made arrangements that, when they died, their slaves would be freed. The death of a master was a slave's only hope for freedom. Slaves who ran away were severely punished if they were caught. Those who revolted against their masters were sometimes killed. Although some masters were kind and fair, others treated their slaves like animals.

*Slaves lived in cabins or huts that stood in a row away from the master's home. These buildings were called the **slave quarters** or **slave row**. Slaves slept on straw mattresses on the floor. Many became sick from the poor and crowded living conditions.*

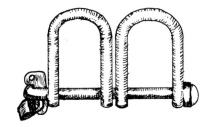

Pieces of property

Because slaves were thought of as property, they were not allowed to learn reading and writing. People believed that the less slaves knew, the easier it was for them to live as slaves. If they could not read, they would not get ideas about living free lives. Some slaves, however, learned to read and write in secret.

Slaves who did not follow rules or work hard and those who tried to run away were cruelly punished. Fifty to one hundred lashes with a long, leather whip was a typical punishment. The hands and legs of runaway slaves were sometimes placed in shackles such as the ones shown above. Shackles did not allow slaves to move.

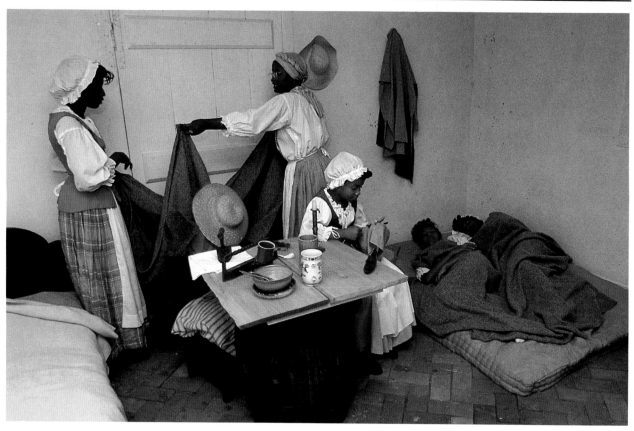

Colonial homes

Some of the very first colonists lived in caves that were dug into hillsides. Others lived in mud huts or cabins made of rough logs. There was usually only one room in the early colonial house. Near the fireplace was a bench, a warm place for people to sit in cold weather. Some families had a table, wooden chairs, and a large chest for bedding and other cloth items. The colonists sat on barrels and slept on straw mattresses.

More comfortable houses

As soon as the settlers had proper materials, they built more comfortable homes, similar to the ones they had left behind in Europe. The English colonists constructed homes of wooden boards cut by hand or in a sawmill. The houses had two stories, winding stairways, large stone chimneys,

The first settlers lived in very simple homes made of logs and mud. There was a fireplace in each home for cooking and keeping warm. Sometimes there was a chimney but, most often, there was just a hole in the roof to allow the smoke to leave the cabin. The colonists soon built better homes, but the living conditions of the slaves (top picture) did not improve.

Some colonists were wealthy and lived in large homes. Their meals were served to them in their dining rooms.

and small windows. Many colonial homes had a parlor, dining room, several bedrooms, and a number of outbuildings, called **dependencies**, which included smokehouses, servants' quarters, and outdoor toilets called **necessaries**. In the southern colonies, the kitchen was located in an outbuilding, thereby keeping the main house free of smoke, odors, fires, and extra heat in summer.

The southern plantation owners built huge homes of brick.

A four-poster bed

Fine furniture

Wealthy colonists had finely designed furniture. Elegant tables, chairs, beds, chests, sofas, clocks, and mirrors filled their houses. Some slept in **four-poster** beds with a tall post at each corner, an overhead covering, and curtains that could be drawn together to keep out cold air. Their mattresses were stuffed with feathers.

Settlements to towns

Whether they lived in the southern or northern colonies, most of the early colonists were farmers. They fed their families by growing crops and raising livestock. They built their own homes and made their own clothing, shoes, and furniture. As more people moved into an area, craftspeople came and opened shops. They made shoes, furniture, barrels, wagons, and horseshoes for the farmers and other people in the community.

Not everyone was a farmer or craftsperson. After a gristmill was built, a miller was hired to grind grain into flour for the people in the area. Others made their living as fishermen, lumberjacks, and shipbuilders. Colonial women who had no husbands supported themselves by working in shops or by sewing for other colonists.

(top) The colonists raised cows for milk, chickens for eggs, and sheep for wool. The farmer above milks his cow, but soon this chore will be done by his young daughters who are standing beside him.

(bottom) Merchants bought goods made in Europe and sold them to the colonists. They also sold products made in the colonies.

The marketplace

Each town had a marketplace where merchants and farmers came to sell their goods or services. During the harvest season in autumn, some markets were open as many as six days a week. Settlers from surrounding farms left home before dawn, their carts and wagons filled with fruits, vegetables, eggs, meat, and homemade products such as baskets, quilts, and hats. They had to arrive early to claim a good spot in the square.

The marketplace was a busy, noisy area. Public notices and announcements were made, and elections were held there. Lawyers and businessmen set up booths in which they offered advice or advertised their services. People could dance or watch puppet shows, cockfights, or horse races. Slave auctions also took place in the busy market square.

(top) As well as produce, handmade items such as men's hats could be bought at the market.

(bottom) The man in the picture is narrating a puppet show. Slave auctions and cockfights were also held in the marketplace.

Questions and answers about colonial life

How did the colonists stay clean?
The colonists believed that bathing too often was bad for one's health. Bathing was believed to rob the skin of precious oils that protected a person from diseases. The colonists only bathed a few times each year, but they did wash each day. Bedrooms contained washing bowls and pitchers of cold water for washing.

Colonists got a lot of cavities because they did not brush their teeth. In those days, teeth could not be filled, so many were pulled out. Some people put cork balls into their mouths to fill in the hollows in their cheeks caused by too many missing teeth!

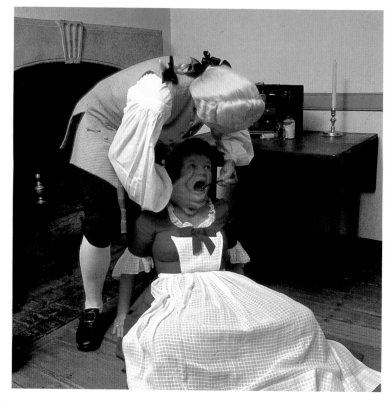

Where was food stored?
Since the colonists had no refrigerators, they needed a cool place to keep their food supplies. They kept food cool in their cellars. The cellars of colonial homes were below ground, as our basements are, but they were not connected to the rest of the house. They had outside entrances. Two large slanting doors led to each cellar.

How were fires put out?

There were no fire departments in colonial days. If there was a fire, everyone in town rushed to help put it out. Those who had firebuckets brought them to the fire. The townspeople organized a bucket brigade by lining up in two rows from the fire to a nearby pond, river, or well. Buckets of water were passed quickly from person to person up the row called the **wet lane.** *Empty buckets were passed down the other row, or* **dry lane,** *to be filled again.*

How was the news spread?

Instead of newspapers, the people of colonial towns depended on the **town crier** *to tell them the important news of the day. His job was to walk through the streets ringing a bell to get people's attention. Then he shouted, or cried out, the news. He did not give details—only a short, simple statement of what had happened.*

Why did the colonists build fences?

(picture opposite page) In some colonial towns, it was the law to enclose one's yard with a fence. Fences were meant to keep animals from straying into private yards. Fences kept animals out but did not stop them from wandering through the streets of the town. (below) In order to keep a gate closed, the colonists attached a chain with a heavy metal ball to the gate. When the gate was opened, the weight of the ball pulled the gate shut.

The colonial family

Colonial families were large. There were several children, and sometimes aunts, uncles, and grandparents all lived under one roof. Everyone worked hard. Fathers and older sons hunted wild birds and animals for meat. They planted and harvested crops or worked at a trade. Mothers, aunts, and grandmothers were busy in the house and garden. They took care of the children and made the family's candles and soap. They spun yarn or thread with a spinning wheel and wove the thread into cloth on a wooden loom.

Lots of work for children

Colonial boys and girls were taught that they should always be eager for work because laziness was a sin. Whether they lived on a farm or in town, they got up early to do chores such as sweeping, feeding chickens, milking cows, watering horses, gathering eggs, picking berries, and running errands.

Learning by working

Not many children had the opportunity to go to school. Boys usually learned their fathers' trades. If a father was a farmer, however, and his son wanted to be a craftsman, the boy could be **apprenticed** to a cooper, wheelwright, or silversmith. He could learn to make barrels, wagon wheels, or fine silver objects in exchange for helping the craftsman who trained him. Boys as young as nine years old became apprentices. They trained for up to seven years.

Sewing samplers

Young girls were taught needlecrafts such as knitting and sewing. When a girl had enough sewing practice, she began work on a **sampler**, which was a sample of her skill in sewing. On a piece of material, the girl sketched a pattern that included short sentences or verses. She was proud when she finished embroidering the pattern with colorful threads of silk or cotton.

Young boys and girls had many chores such as milking cows and feeding chickens.

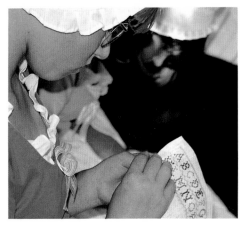

The girl in the picture above is sewing a sampler containing letters of the alphabet. Verses from the Bible were also sewn on samplers.

15

a flowering tobacco plant

Celia's family

My name is Celia, and I am a slave. I was brought to Virginia by slave ship from Africa. I am the property of Mr. Stell, a wealthy tobacco plantation owner. My husband's name is Felix.

Felix and I have three children. Our children are also slaves. Felix and our son Jeremiah work in the fields picking tobacco. They work hard from sunup to sundown with only fifteen minutes a day for rest. I am Mr. Stell's cook. My younger children, who are ten and eight, help me in the kitchen. They pick vegetables from the garden, fetch water from the well, churn butter, and wash dishes. Mr. Stell expects us all to work hard. He tells us that it costs a lot of money to keep slaves.

You probably wonder if I am happy. My mother always told me there was nothing to be happy about when you were a slave, but life is too short to be walking around always fussing and feuding. Sometimes I think about my life as a child in Africa. It is hard for me to understand how some white folks can treat us black folks so badly because our skins are a different color. Sometimes I rebel quietly by burning supper or spilling food into the fire, but last week I got a whipping, so this week I am doing my best to cook good meals.

I am happy when dinner is finished because I have some time to spend with my family. Felix and I tell stories to our children. We want them to know who they are and where they came from. We hope they will tell their children stories about our families in Africa. Sometimes we sing and Felix plays his drum.

It is almost Christmas, a happy time for slaves. If we are lucky, we will get a week off. Sometimes the Stells give us a Christmas box of clothes and some sweet biscuits for our children. But New Year's Day is just around the corner, and it is a sad time for many slaves, including us. Mr. Stell needs money, so he will be selling my older son, Jeremiah. I don't know if we will ever see him again. That is a very hard thing for slaves—to be separated from their families. But white folks don't consider our feelings. They don't think of us as people—we are just their property!

Celia's family lives in the slave quarters of the plantation. Celia is carding wool, Felix is beside her, and Jeremiah is in the front of the picture. The younger children are shown in the picture below. Felix's brother and his wife also share the cabin with Celia's family. Slaves had very little comfort or privacy in their living quarters.

Celia's younger son and daughter are enjoying their Christmas treat of sweet biscuits. They are happy to have a special treat but are sad to think that their older brother Jeremiah will soon be sold. They may never see him again!

Children at school

There were very few free schools in the colonies. When there was a school in town, the children who could afford to attend had classes six days a week. There was only one teacher, and all the students learned their lessons in the same room. Some children studied quietly, while others recited out loud. Students were taught to read, write, and **cipher**, or solve simple arithmetic problems. They learned by repeating their lessons over and over. Students who misbehaved were given a whipping!

Very few learning materials

Schools usually had only two books—a Bible and a **primer** that contained the alphabet, spelling words, and poems. Young students learned their letters and numbers from a **hornbook**, which hung from their belts. Some children had **copy books** made of paper that was bound together with thread. Students drew lines on each page with a ruler and wrote in small handwriting. They did this in order to save paper, which was hard to get in the colonies.

Higher education for boys only

Girls did not attend high school because they were expected to stay home and run a household. Of the boys who completed high school, a few went on to universities in England or to one of the nine colleges in the colonies. Most of these colleges were started by churches to train young men to become ministers.

an inkwell and feather quill

A hornbook was like a wooden paddle to which a piece of paper was attached. The letters of the alphabet, numbers, and a prayer or verse from the Bible were printed on the paper, which was covered by a thin sheet of horn. Students used their hornbooks to help them learn their letters and numbers.

Students practiced their hand-writing in copy books. They wrote by dipping a feather quill into ink.

Outdoor bowling is lots of fun!

To play marbles, you draw a circle around a hoop and place a marble inside the circle. Everyone takes turns trying to hit the marble. When someone misses, his or her marble stays inside the circle. The one who hits the center marble wins all the marbles in the circle.

Quoits *is played by trying to toss a ring on top of a stake called a* **hob.**

Children at play

Children did not have much time for play but, when they did, they took part in simple pleasures such as walking on stilts, spinning tops, and rolling hoops. Outdoors, they bowled, played **quoits**, marbles, or a game of cricket, which is a little like baseball. They flew kites, enjoyed a game of Blindman's Buff, ran sack races, or went fishing. Both boys and girls enjoyed board games. A favorite board game was The Game of Goose. One could also be pushed on a swing, sit on a seesaw with a sister, or just lie in the grass and chat with friends.

The people in the picture above are wearing their best clothes. Their suits and dresses are made of silk, brocade, and lace. The men's coats are embroidered with shiny threads. In those days, both men and women wore wigs, although, in the picture, only the men are wearing them.

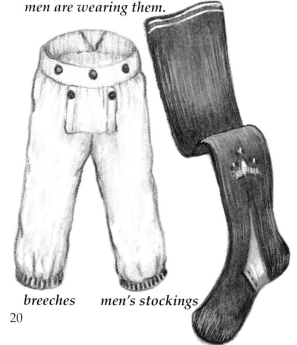

breeches   men's stockings

Men's clothing

The fashions of two hundred years ago were different from those of today. Men did not wear long pants. Their pants, called **breeches**, reached just below their knees. Breeches had buttons because zippers had not yet been invented. Woolen stockings were worn beneath the breeches.

Fancy suits

Men's shirts were loose fitting and sometimes had ruffles at the neck and cuffs. **Waistcoats** were worn over the shirts. A waistcoat is a long vest with buttons. Men's suit coats reached the knees and had large cuffs. On their feet, men wore boots or shoes that were identical. There was no left or right shoe or boot.

The man in the top left picture is wearing a loose gown, called a **banyan**, over his shirt and breeches. Banyans were worn outdoors in the summer or indoors anytime. The soft hat he is wearing was often worn at home instead of a wig.

(top right) Some men wore cloaks over their waistcoats. Hats were worn every day. Some were small, some had wide brims, and some had three corners.

The man in the picture on the left belongs to the working class. He is not wealthy. His clothes are plain and made of wool. His three-cornered hat is called a **tricorne**.

a tricorne

Pockets were not attached to clothes. They could be reached through slits in the skirt.

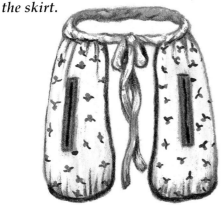

Pocket-hoop farthingales *made women's waists look thin and gave their stomachs a flat appearance.*

Women's fashions

The clothing worn by the women of the eighteenth century was beautiful but not very comfortable or practical. Dresses were long, and underneath there were several layers of petticoats. Women who worked around the home or in a shop wore simple dresses made of wool, linen, or cotton. They protected their clothing with aprons. They had to make sure their dresses did not get dirty. Most people only had two sets of clothes—one for weekdays and one for Sundays.

Little comfort, lots of pain!

Wealthy women wore clothes made of silk or brocade, with lace ruffles peeking out at the neck and from under the sleeves. It was fashionable to have small waists, so women wore corsets under their clothes. The corsets, called **stays**, were laced so tightly that women could hardly breathe!

Both men and women wore wigs. More than one hundred styles of wigs were created in colonial days. An expensive wig cost as much as housing and feeding a servant for one year. People paid a yearly fee to have their heads shaved and their wigs powdered, curled, and combed regularly.

calash

A **calash** was like the top of a convertible car. It was collapsible. It covered and protected big hairdos and wigs from the wind and rain.

Look at the dress on the right. It has a low neckline and sleeves that reach the elbows with frills showing below them. The **bodice** of the dress is tight. It is stiffened with whalebone and open in front to show an embroidered **stomacher**. A petticoat is worn under the dress and can be seen underneath the open skirt. It is made from two layers of material that are quilted together. Pocket hoops are worn under the skirt. The skirt is separate from the bodice.

Women wore clogs over their shoes to protect the shoes from getting muddy on dirt roads.

clog

Women wore hooded cloaks to keep them warm and to cover their hair and dress. They warmed their hands inside muffs.

cloak

wig

stomacher

bodice

muff

The colonists traveled by boat, wagon, or stagecoach, such as the one shown above. They stayed overnight at inns or taverns. Besides lodging, taverns also offered dinner and entertainment. Sometimes parties and balls were held there.

Travel, transportation, and taverns

Most early colonists did not venture far from home. Only government officials, merchants, and planters traveled for business or pleasure. The best way to get from one place to another was on a river, lake, or along the seacoast by boat.

Land travel

Travel on land was slow and difficult. The first colonial roads were paths that followed old Indian trails through the woods. The only way to travel these roads was on foot. Although colonists widened the paths for travel with carts or wagons, many wooden bridges could be used only by foot travelers.

By the middle of the eighteenth century, roads had improved so that colonists could ride in carriages or coaches drawn by four to eight horses. There were no trains or automobiles; colonial stagecoaches took passengers from one settlement to another. Open or covered wagons were used to transport goods.

Food and rest

Inns and taverns provided food and lodging for stagecoach and riverboat passengers. After a meal and hot drink in the tavern, a traveler went upstairs to an unheated room where he slept in a bed with one or two people he had never met before. Rooms often had more than one bed, no lock on the door, and slept four to six people. Servants and slaves slept in the barn with the horses. The few women who traveled lodged with families in the community.

Renting a bedroom in colonial days meant renting "room in bed." Four to six men slept in a small room. Beds had straw mattresses that rested on woven ropes. The sheets were seldom clean.

Work and fun

Colonists seldom had time just for pleasure. They often combined work with fun. They enjoyed working together raising houses, plowing fields, husking corn, sewing quilts, and making cider. There was always plenty of food to eat when the work was done. Sometimes people danced after the meal. The settlers kicked up their heels doing reels, jigs, and square dances.

The pastimes of the wealthy

Wealthy colonists had servants or slaves to do their jobs for them while they enjoyed themselves reading, playing musical instruments, or entertaining guests with charades, board games, card games, and chess. They had formal parties at which ladies and gentlemen danced the **minuet**. In Williamsburg, Virginia, fancy parties were held at the Governor's Palace. Only the most important people in the colonies were invited to dine and dance with the Governor!

A colonial Christmas

The colonists celebrated some holidays, but not in the same way we celebrate them. A colonial Christmas, for example, was not like Christmas today. The first colonists did not take time away from their work to celebrate this holiday. In some colonies, celebrating Christmas was forbidden because people did not believe that it was a truly Christian holiday. In later days, colonists had simple Christmas celebrations with small gifts for their children, a few decorations, and special foods such as plum pudding.

Many men came to help out at a house raising. The women cooked a huge meal. Everyone enjoyed the party that followed.

Fancy parties and balls were held at the Governor's Palace in Williamsburg, the capital city of Virginia. People wore their finest clothes at these functions. An orchestra played for the guests.

Christmas decorations were simple, such as this fruit wreath hanging outside a colonial home. Sometimes groups of people visited their friends and sang Christmas carols for them. The carolers were invited inside for a hot drink and some refreshments.

Stories and songs from Africa

Although slaves worked hard and had difficult lives, even they found ways to enjoy themselves. When they came home from the fields, they gathered around a campfire to share stories and music. They taught and entertained their children with **folktales**, which are stories that include a **moral**, or a belief, about good and evil. An older person told the story, and listeners joined in by singing and dancing.

Slaves spent Sundays and holidays with their families and friends, making music and singing. They sang happy songs and sad songs. Music was an important part of their lives because it was one of the few ways that slaves could express their feelings.

Homemade instruments

The slaves did not have the musical instruments used in Africa, so they found other ways to make musical sounds. To make a drum, goat or sheep skin was tied across a dried, hollowed-out gourd or a small barrel. Bison horns made excellent flutes, and dried animal bones were used as drumsticks. Old cowbells made a great sound when struck with a stick.

African rhythms

It was a special time for the slaves when they were able to sit together and sing African songs and new **spirituals**, or religious songs, they had learned in America. The words of the songs were not as important as their rhythms. To help themselves keep up a quick pace, field workers often chanted rhythms while working.

The slaves played homemade instruments such as drums, cowbells, shaken sekeres, and slit drums. Slit drums were blocks of wood with slits through their sides. Sekeres (pronounced shake-a-rays) were made from dried gourds, which are hard-shelled fruits. Hard, dried nuts, beans, and seeds were tied onto a net and then put around the gourd. When shaken, this musical instrument made a very loud sound.

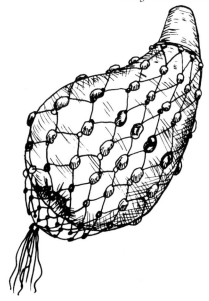

An example of a rhythm:
The big bee flies high
The little bee makes the honey
The black folks make the cotton
The white folks get the money.

Prejudice

So many slaves were brought to America from Africa that, in some colonies, more than half the population was black. African Americans were not treated like human beings because of the color of their skin. This simple difference led to **prejudice**. Prejudice is a strong feeling or judgment made about someone merely because of his or her race, religion, or background.

The slave traders of colonial times created a **myth**, which is a false belief, that the native Africans were inferior to white people. Slavery lasted three hundred years in North America. Many white people thought it was wrong and fought to put an end to it. In the year 1865, laws were passed to end slavery in the United States.

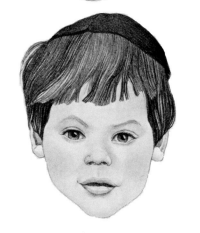

Although slavery was stopped, prejudice against African Americans continued. African Americans could not go to the same schools, use the same washrooms, or work at the same jobs as white Americans. Throughout history, African Americans and people of other racial and ethnic backgrounds have suffered from hateful words, harmful acts, and other types of discrimination.

Fighting prejudice

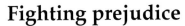

Prejudice hurts everyone. Nothing good can come of it. Are you prejudiced against someone because of his or her race, religion, or background? Have you tried to be friends with that person? How can you change your thinking and behavior?

Glossary

apprentice One who is learning a trade under a skilled craftsperson

brocade A heavy woven fabric with a raised design

carding The combing of fibers to prepare them for spinning

cipher To do simple arithmetic

cockfight A fight between two roosters

colonist A person who lives in a colony

colony A territory inhabited by settlers who are governed by a distant country

cooper A person who makes barrels, buckets, and tubs

craftspeople People skilled in creating handmade goods

cricket A game played on a grass field with a ball, bats, and wickets. It is played by two teams of eleven players each.

embroidery The art of decorating with designs in needlework

folktale A story that is handed down from generation to generation

gourd A hard-shelled fruit that grows on a vine

gristmill A mill for grinding grain

harvest The time of year when ripened crops are gathered

jig A fast, lively dance

merchant A storekeeper or one who trades goods

minuet A slow and graceful dance

moral A lesson about right and wrong

New World A term used by Europeans to refer to North America in its early days of settlement

overseer A person who directs the work of laborers or slaves

parlor A special room in which guests are entertained

plantation A large farm where crops, such as cotton, tobacco, or sugar are grown

planter A plantation owner

primer A first book for teaching children to read

produce Farm products, especially fresh fruits and vegetables

quill A pen made from the hollow stem of a feather

reel A folk dance in which two or more couples form two lines facing each other

settlement A small established community

silversmith A person who makes things out of silver

smokehouse A building in which meat or fish is treated with smoke to preserve and flavor it

square dance A dance performed by groups of four or more couples who are arranged in a square at the beginning of the dance

trade Something that a person does to earn a living

wheelwright A person who makes or repairs wheels or wheeled vehicles

working class Those people who work with their hands and are dependent upon wages for their livelihood. People who are neither rich nor poor

Index

Africa 6, 16, 17, 29, 30

apprentices 15

bathing 12

bedrooms 9, 12

boats 25

bowling 19

breeches 20

caroling 27

Celia's family 16-17

cellars 12

children 10, 14, 15, 16, 17, 18-19, 26, 29

chores 15

Christmas 17, 26, 27

clothing 20-23, 27

corsets 22

craftspeople 10, 15

dancing 26, 27

dresses 22, 23

families 14-17

farmers 10, 11, 13, 15

fences 13

fires 13

folktales 29

food 12

four-poster beds 9

fun 19, 26

games 19, 26

gardens 13

gates 13

Governor's Palace 26, 27

gristmill 10

homes 8-9

hornbook 18

house raising 26

inns 24-25

Jamestown 5

kitchens 9

marbles 19

marketplace 11, 13

merchants 10, 11, 25

music 17, 29

musical instruments 26, 29

news 13

outbuildings 9

plantations 5, 6, 7, 9, 16, 17

prejudice 30

puppet show 11

questions and answers 12-13

quoits 19

roads 25

samplers 15

schools 15, 18

shackles 7

shaken sekeres 29

slave quarters 7, 17

slave traders 6, 30

slaves 6-7, 8, 11, 16, 17, 25, 26, 29, 30

spinning 15

stagecoach 24

stockings 20

taverns 24-25

teeth 12

Thirteen Colonies 4, 5

toilets 9

tops 19

town crier 13

travel 24-25

tricornes 21

Virginia 5, 16, 26, 27

wigs 20, 21, 23

Williamsburg 26, 27

4 5 6 7 8 9 0 Printed in USA 1 0 9 8 7 6 5